Other books in the series:

Prophet Muhammad ﷺ

Abu Bakr as-Siddiq ﷺ

Umar ibn al-Khattab ﷺ

Uthman ibn Affan ﷺ

Hasan and Husayn İbn Ali ﷺ

Aisha bint Abu Bakr ﷺ

Fatima ﷺ bint Muhammad ﷺ

Khalid ibn al-Walid ﷺ

THE AGE OF BLISS

KHADIJA رضي الله عنها
BINT KHUWAYLID

MEHMET BÜYÜKŞAHİN

NEW JERSEY • LONDON • FRANKFURT • CAIRO • JAKARTA

TUGHRA
BOOKS

New Jersey

Translated by Asiye Gülen
Editen by Clare Duman

Published by Tughra Books
335 Clifton Ave., Clifton,
NJ, 07011, USA

www.tughrabooks.com

Library of Congress Cataloging-in-Publication Data Available

ISBN: 978-1-59784-375-1

TABLE OF CONTENTS

Khadija bint Khuwaylid ﷺ

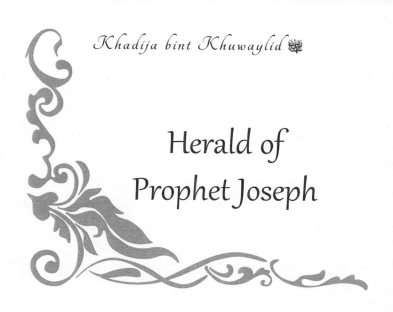

Herald of
Prophet Joseph

wo men wandered through a beautiful green garden, in between the date trees groaning under the weight of their ripe, luscious fruit. Prophet Joseph, peace be upon him, was plucking the large, juicy dates from the trees and putting them into Khuwaylid's gown. Khuwaylid, may Allah be pleased with him, the father of Khadija, held the sides of his gown together like a pouch, but somehow it never filled up.

Picking one of the biggest fruits, Prophet Joseph put it into Khuwaylid's mouth. At that moment, Khuwaylid heard a voice, "O Khuwaylid, wake up!"

Opening his eyes, Khuwaylid understood he had been dreaming. "O Fatima," he called to his wife. "Come close to me. Listen to what I have to tell you."

Fatima, may Allah be pleased with her, came over to Khuwaylid and saw his eyes flickering with happiness as if they were shining in the sunlight. Smiling, she asked, "Tell me what happened. What is the reason for your joy?"

"We will have a son and he will bring abundance to our home. His name will be widespread throughout the land. I will name him Joseph and he will be as virtuous and benign as Prophet Joseph."

Listening to her husband, Fatima remained silent. Khuwaylid was surprised at her lack of interest. Looking into her eyes he asked, "O Fatima, doesn't this news make you happy?"

Fatima had a good heart and never wished anyone to be sad. "My dear husband," she replied, "I wish for everything that you tell me to come true. But, the date fruit in your dream indicates a girl. I believe we will have a daughter."

Khuwaylid's shoulders dropped. He looked pleadingly at his wife, "If we have a girl, what will my father say to me? How could I walk through the streets and face people?"

Fatima's heart sank. Her eyes filling with tears she said, "Not every dream comes true. We must be prepared for either a girl or a boy."

Khuwaylid stood up and wandered around the room restlessly, pausing to look out of the window. Turning to Fatima, he sighed, "Would you bury your daughter alive?"

"What are you saying Khuwaylid?" Fatima cried. "No matter whether it's a boy or a girl, I will protect it with my own life."

Khuwaylid was a good hearted, righteous, and benevolent man, but he felt uneasy regarding the community. "I feel the same and I agree with you. But what about our traditions and customs?"

Fatima was speechless; she didn't know how to reply. Her head was filled with a buzzing noise and tears ran unchecked down her cheeks. Turning to Khuwaylid, she demanded, "Didn't a woman give birth to you?"

"Of course, you are right," he responded, "but I want my first child to be a boy."

Fatima knew well the rules of the desert. "Don't be unhappy, Khuwaylid," she said, "Our child will be a good person."

Khuwaylid was filled with emotion. Terrible memories of girls being buried alive filled his mind. Bowing his head, he murmured, "There's no conscience anymore. People are ignorant. My father wants me to have a son to continue his line of descendants. He will never allow people to say, 'Look, Asad had a granddaughter.'"

Softly, Fatima tried to reason with Khuwaylid, "I feel we will have a daughter and she will soften the hearts of all who see her, because she is the harbinger of Prophet Joseph."

Fatima's words brought some comfort to Khuwaylid who was pleased with her interpretation of the dream. He looked at her and smiled.

Her Name Should Be Khadija

Time passed and soon Fatima began to get birthing pains. According to their calculations, it was not yet time for the baby to arrive. It was early. The whole family descended into panic; would the child be stillborn?

Khuwaylid informed their relatives and soon the house was filled with his uncle, sibling, father and neighbors. Khuwaylid's nephew, Waraqa ibn Nawfal, may Allah be pleased with him, also arrived with his sister. Everyone was in a state of excitement.

Preparations were begun; if the baby were a boy, there would be a huge celebration. But, Khuwaylid stayed out of the way and spoke to no one, as if he had swallowed his tongue.

It was nearly evening time and everyone was becoming restless. All eyes were on the door of the birthing room, waiting for any news from inside. Finally, the moment came. Leaving the room, and making her way through the hustle and bustle, a mid-wife approached Khuwaylid's father, Asad, a look of shame on her face. "A healthy girl has been born and her mother, Fatima, is also well."

Hearing the news at the same time as the others, Khuwaylid was very upset. He had been expecting a son. His face reddened as if guilty of a crime. He felt like crying and disappeared behind the house. Leaning against the wall and looking at the camels in the courtyard, Khuwaylid was in the depths of despair. He was roused by the voice of his slave, calling him to visit the mother as tradition dictated.

Waraqa, Asad and Khuwaylid entered Fatima's room together, each of them looking unhappy. Lying in bed, Fatima held the baby in her arms. With one look at the child, Asad's gloomy face lit up and at that moment his heart softened and his eyes sparkled. He turned back to his guests and announced the good news, "We have been blessed with a baby girl. She will bring happiness and abundance to our house. I invite you to the table to eat and celebrate with us."

Everyone one in the room stood still in shock, the looks on their faces souring. Such a reaction from Asad was not expected. There was only one person who was delighted by this declaration. Khuwaylid felt as if a weight had been lifted from his shoulders. He had only wished for a son to make his father happy. After the dream, he had known his baby would be a girl. He smiled broadly and kissed the hand of his father.

Waraqa, unable to hold back any longer, came to the middle of the room and asked for the baby to be brought to him. Holding the innocent baby in his arms, he smiled and said, "Her name should be Khadija. She was born earlier than expected and she is a cotton-white baby."

Giving a short speech, he prayed that the name would bring good luck and happiness to the baby.

Honorable Visitor

After the name-giving ceremony only a few people remained in the house, just a handful of women along with Asad and Waraqa. One of the women announced that Abdul Muttalib, may Allah be pleased with him, was coming. The leader of the Quraysh tribe and the person who had rediscovered the Zamzam well, his visit was a great honor for the house of Khuwaylid. Everyone rushed to the door to welcome him.

Abdul Muttalib stood for a while in the courtyard and looked at his surroundings. Entering the house, he drank from the caudle offered to him and talked about Khadija. Waraqa also joined them.

Abdul Muttalib said, "I see that for the first time people are smiling after the birth of a girl. I also feel very comfortable."

Raising his head, Asad looked at the sky. The air was clear and the stars shone around the full moon. Smiling, he answered, "O leader, I also thought that I would go mad when a girl was born. But this was not the case."

Abdul Muttalib began to wonder about Khadija. "I want to see this baby," he requested.

They all entered the birth room where little Khadija lay in her cot. The candles burning beside her bed lent a glow to the air that further enhanced her beauty. Picking up the baby, Abdul Muttalib lifted her into the air. She was a light as a feather and as soft as a cloud.

Abdul Muttalib was confused. In his whole life he had never seen a baby who shone so brightly. Suddenly, the money he had brought as a gift seemed inadequate for such a child. He emptied his pockets leaving everything he had beside the cot. The people around him were astonished. Usually such a large gift would be reserved for a baby boy. His behavior moved those who witnessed it. Khuwaylid approached his daughter and gazed at her with unending affection.

After leaving his gifts for baby Khadija, Abdul Muttalib left the house. His visit had been a great honor and had delighted the family, particularly Khuwaylid. According to tradition, such visits were only made when a boy was born.

And so, with the birth of little Khadija, some of the old traditions began to change. Both Khuwaylid and Fatima were full of joy. Khadija was the font of happiness for their house.

When she was three months old, little Khadija was given to the care of a wet nurse, as was the tradition in those days. For a few years, the nurse would raise her before returning her to her parents.

The Children

K hadija's parents did everything in their power to give her a good upbringing. It was Khuwaylid's wish for Waraqa to educate his daughter and he asked Fatima her opinion. Agreeing with her husband, they went to visit Waraqa.

Waraqa immediately accepted their offer and they began with the lessons. Khadija was a bright and diligent student who learned to read and write easily. Her intelligence fascinated Waraqa. In those days, girls were rarely educated and were usually forced to work like slaves. Most men couldn't read and write so for Khadija this was an important privilege.

As well as learning to read and write, Khadija learned many things from Waraqa. Soon people began to notice her good manners and beauty and, before she was even mature, she started to attract marriage proposals, each of which she rejected.

By the age of fifteen, Khadija had grown into a well-behaved young lady and was renowned for her cleanliness and good manners. Deciding that she was old enough to get married, her parents started to research possible candidates. Khadija rejected them all, but the last one, Abu Hala, was not so easy to reject, as he was beloved and respected by all.

Approaching her daughter, Fatima said, "My dear, Abu Hala wants to marry you."

Khadija bowed her head. Abu Hala was the son of a wealthy and noble Meccan family. He was honest and honorable and known to be hard-working.

"What does my father say about this matter?" Khadija replied.

"Your father agrees."

"Then, it will be as you wish. But first, I would like to ask Waraqa, son of my uncle. I can't make a decision without asking him."

Fatima was relieved. "Of course," she said, "You have thought well. We wouldn't promise anything without asking him."

Khadija asked, "Can I go and ask him now?" and receiving her mother's permission, she ran to Waraqa's side.

Seeing his cousin running towards him, Waraqa said, "O Khadija, you look so distressed. What has happened?"

"O cousin, Abu Hala wants to marry me," wailed Khadija. "My parents also want that. Can you allow me to marry him?"

Waraqa answered in a fatherly manner, "He is a good man, Khadija. He is rich, honest and noble. If your parents agree, you should accept his proposal."

Khadija was silent, lost in thought. Looking at her, Waraqa said firmly, "You marry him and I will solemnize your wedding."

So, Khadija married Abu Hala when she was fifteen years old. The marriage only lasted two years before Abu Hala unfortunately died. Khadija was left with two children and a huge fortune.

Left to look after herself, Khadija decided to try her hand at trade. She prepared some caravans and sent them to nearby cities. Her skill as a business-woman earned her a lot of money in just a short time and she became one of the elite women of Mecca and the envy of many of the main Meccan businessmen.

Khadija's exceptional talent, intelligence, geniali-ty and fairness attracted a lot of attention and she was soon the receiver of many marriage proposals. Khad-ija rejected all these proposals but when she received one from Atiq, a noble, honest, rich and industrious man, she decided to give it some thought.

Khadija sought the advice of her parents and other elder relatives about Atiq's proposal. Their verdict was unanimously favorable; they all agreed it would be a respectable and correct match. So, at sev-enteen years old, Khadija married Atiq and was blessed with a daughter from this marriage. Howev-er, as with her first marriage, this one was not to last long. After the birth of his child, Atiq travelled with his caravan on a long journey, but never returned. Khadija received the news that she had again been widowed. She decided to think no more about mar-riage and to concentrate on business.

The Dawn in Mecca
Is Imminent

The Arabian Peninsula was a place where you could find rich people living in abundance and luxury whilst the poor could barely find a slice of bread to eat. Khadija was one of the rich, but she lived a simple life, running her household and looking after her children herself. When her caravans arrived in Mecca, the poor and the orphans would surround the camels, waiting for some charity. Khadija was the hope of the poor and the protector of the orphans.

When she was thirty-four, Khadija's father was killed in a war. This sorry event was followed not long after by the death of her mother. Khadija keenly felt the loss of these two important people. With few people around her to share her grief and problems, Waraqa became her main source of support. Without him she would have been utterly alone.

At nearly eighty years old, Waraqa was nearly blind. Whenever Khadija felt lonely, she would visit him and it was during these visits that Waraqa would tell her about the foretold last Prophet who was heralded in the holy books. Waraqa believed that the time of the last Prophet was imminent.

Captivated by this news, Khadija spent long hours thinking about it and soon her dreams were filled with the last Prophet. One night she had a dream, but this time it was different from the others.

In her dream, a star broke away from the sky, entered her chest and came out of her arms. It ascended into the sky and drowned everything in light. Waking and realizing it was just a dream, she felt very sad. "Such beauty is only found in dreams," she thought.

Slowly rising from her bed, Khadija went to her window. As though wanting to fly away, she threw open the shutters and looked up at the sky. The air was clear and the stars were flickering. She looked for the star of her dream, but all the stars here looked the same; there was no difference between them.

"It's almost dawn. In the morning I can visit Waraqa and he will be able to interpret my dream," she thought.

When the sun appeared on the horizon, Khadija prepared herself and left her house to visit Waraqa. Seeing her excitement, he asked, "What has happened? What makes you so excited?"

Khadija related the details of her dream. Waraqa was stunned and his heart raced. Tears flowed down his cheeks. Calmly, he addressed his cousin, "Khadija, this is a beautiful message for you. This dream is obviously a gift to you. Your house will be filled with a holy light. Only the Creator knows the truth, but this holy light will be the light of the noble Prophet."

Gaping at Waraqa with wide eyes, Khadija was nearly paralyzed by what she heard. "What has this to do with me?" she asked, looking enquiringly at her cousin.

"The last Prophet is among us," continued Waraqa.

Khadija's heart almost stopped. She was so excited. Waraqa explained everything as if reading from a book. Speaking slowly and clearly, he said, "He is from the Quraysh which is the tribe of Hashim's sons. You are going to be his wife!"

Khadija couldn't believe what she was hearing. She repeated the words in her mind, 'You are going to be his wife!' What did this mean? Had she heard correctly? She asked Waraqa with curiosity, "Am I really going to be his wife?"

"Yes, my dear Khadija," he answered. "You are the life partner of the noble Prophet. During your marriage, he will receive the first revelation. You will be the first person to become Muslim. His religion will spread all over the world."

Khadija was tempted to say, 'I am not thinking of marrying again,' but she held her tongue. She remembered her dream of the previous night. What would it be like, to be the wife of a Prophet?

Waraqa could almost read her heart. He continued to explain the characteristics of the noble Prophet. "He is absolutely not unscrupulous. He does not yell, scream, or shout. He never reciprocates evil with evil. He has abundant forgiveness and mercy."

Khadija was shocked. Everything she knew from experience seemed wiped away. "O my dear cousin," she stuttered, "How do you know all of this?"

In fact, Khadija already knew the answer to this question. She had heard it many times when she was Waraqa's student. She could never forget this; she was very smart. But at that moment, everything had been wiped from her mind. So, Waraqa began to explain everything again, as if it was the first time. "The Torah and the Gospel inform us about his coming."

Khadija listened carefully, then she asked another question, "You describe him as if he were standing now in front of you. Tell me more about what he will look like."

"I read in the Gospel that he shouldn't be short. He is medium-sized with white skin, and he has the Prophet's sign between his two shoulders. He doesn't accept any alms. He rides on donkeys and camels. He is a shepherd and milks the sheep. He wears patched clothes. And his name is Ahmad."

Khadija was over 30 years old. Until her dream, she had rejected all of her many suitors. Now, however, she began in earnest her preparations to marry. She concentrated on developing herself into a worthy wife for the noble Prophet. She devoted her attentions to science and started to learn again from Waraqa, examining the Torah and the Gospel and perfecting her already spotless life.

Like her cousin, Waraqa, Khadija believed in the religion that Abraham had brought; the Hanif religion. Often visiting the Ka'ba to pray to The Unique One, she would become disturbed by the presence of idols and the ignorance of the polytheists.

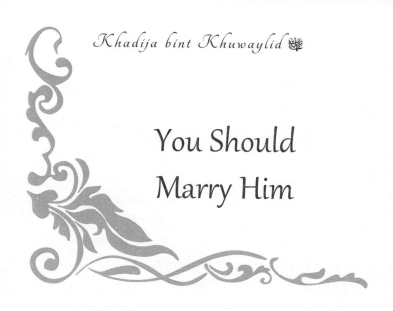

You Should Marry Him

K hadija had made a very good profit from her last caravan. She went to the Ka'ba and gave thanks to Allah. Whilst she was praying, she thought about the poor people who needed help and she asked for their grace. Seeing people sold as if they were objects made her very sad. Circumambulating the Ka'ba, she used to cry for them.

The people in Mecca were waiting for a savior and Khadija believed it would be the last Prophet. In her heart, she wished that she would be his first wife. This would be a great honor for her. However, she didn't think his task of helping the people would be easy. "Your mission is a difficult one, dear Prophet," she thought to herself.

Returning home, she came across some women sitting in the street, chatting to each other freely. Khadija joined them. After a while, a man approached them saying, "O women of Mecca. Without doubt, in the near future a Prophet will appear here. His name is Ahmad. The woman who is here with you shouldn't hesitate to marry him."

Hearing the word "Prophet" made the polytheist women uncomfortable. Some of them threw stones at the man, calling him, "Stupid!" Only Khadija remained still. She understood the meaning of what the man had said. He was talking about the last Prophet from her dream.

Sultan of Dreams

he never-ending tribal wars caused the Meccan people to become poorer and poorer. Khadija had stockpiled many goods and wished to send them to Damascus to sell them. The journey was long and dangerous and she was looking for an honest man to lead the caravan. It should be an honorable person who would protect her reputation.

Abu Talib heard the news that Khadija was looking for a trustworthy leader for her caravan and went hastily to the side of the future Prophet, Muhammad, peace and blessings be upon him.

"O nephew!" he began, "Times are hard and our difficulties are increasing. We are poor and I have no more goods to sell. I am not strong enough to do business. There are some caravans ready to set out for Damascus and the owners are looking for honest leaders. One of them is Khadija, the daughter of Khuwaylid. She is also looking for an honest and loyal leader for her caravan. If you go to her I believe she will accept you."

"Maybe she will send us a note," replied our noble Prophet, peace and blessings be upon him.

"I don't think so," Abu Talib said. "She could give the job to someone else. Let's go and ask for the job immediately."

"As you wish, dear uncle," our Prophet replied.

Atiqa, our noble Prophet's aunt, visited Khadija to request the job on his behalf. Khadija knew of the beloved Prophet's reputation as an honest man with good manners, but she doubted his interest in the job. She immediately sent him a message informing him that the job was his and that she would pay extra to him if it were necessary.

A short while later, our noble Prophet, peace and blessings be upon him, visited Khadija. Upon seeing him, Khadija instantly understood that he was the future Prophet she had been waiting for. After a short silence, they began to speak but the noble Prophet's modesty prevented him from looking at her face directly. Khadija came straight to the point. "I have a caravan ready to set out to Damascus. I have been looking for someone to lead it there and back for a long time. I know that you are an honest man. If you'll accept this job, I'll pay you more than I have ever paid anyone."

Our noble Prophet, peace and blessing be upon him, accepted the offer and went to give the good news to his uncle, Abu Talib. His uncle was very happy and emotional. "O nephew, this is a gift from Allah. I heard that Khadija gives two camels to each of her employees but I think this is not enough for you. I will speak with her regarding this."

Our beloved Prophet looked at his uncle and indicated that he would not interfere.

Understanding his nephew's look, Abu Talib set out to visit Khadija, preparing his arguments in his mind. He would tell her all the good characteristics of his nephew, which were well known by everyone.

Greeting Abu Talib, Khadija invited him to sit in the best place in her house. Abu Talib began to explain why he had come. "Dear Khadija, I have heard that you give each of your employees two camels but this is very little for my nephew who has a very superior character. I came to request double the amount for him."

Khadija looked at Abu Talib. This old man had walked a long way to make this request and he must be tired. She wished to make him comfortable and assured him, "Dear Abu Talib, I find your request to be inadequate. Even this amount is not worthy of Muhammad. It would please me if you asked for more because everyone is aware of his superior characteristics."

Surprised that the bargaining was so easy, Abu Talib came to an agreement with Khadija. Then they discussed the date that the caravan would set out.

The day of departure arrived and Khadija found herself to be unusually excited. Calling her most trusted servant, Maysara, to her side, she instructed, "Listen to me carefully. The leader of the caravan is Muhammad al-Amin (the Trustworthy). Never disobey him and never dissent to any of his ideas."

Maysara was surprised and almost asked the importance of this person. But, Khadija had not finished, "Furthermore, you will report to me everything that he does and everything about his behavior. You will also fulfill some tasks for me."

"Your wish is my command," Maysara replied.

At last, the caravan set out on its long journey from Mecca. The journey to Damascus would take almost three months.

The time for the caravan's return was approaching and every day Khadija climbed to the roof of her house and watched the horizon, waiting impatiently for it to return. Today was different. Time refused to pass. Khadija remained on her roof all day, just waiting and watching. At last, the moment came that she had been waiting so long for; the caravan appeared. However, there was something unusual about it. A small cloud was following the caravan.

When the caravan arrived in Mecca, Khadija immediately called Maysara to her side and asked about the strange cloud. "It was the same for the whole journey," the servant explained.

Khadija took a plate of fresh dates and offered them to our beloved Prophet, peace and blessings be upon him. He ate the fruit with pleasure but the plate never finished. This fact was not lost on Khadija.

First of all, they calculated the profit that the business trip had made. Khadija was aware that the profit was very good, but she wasn't interested in the money. She could only think about her dream and whether Muhammad al-Amin, peace and blessings be upon him, was really the last Prophet that Waraqa had talked about.

Later, Khadija's servant related many more strange events that had happened during the journey. As she listened, Khadija became more and more amazed.

"As soon as the caravan left Mecca I started to fulfill the tasks you set me," Maysara began. "First I asked him to dismount the skinny camel and to wear the clothes you gave me. This made Abu Jahl and Shayba very angry. They complained, 'Why are you showing so much attention to this orphan? Let him wear his old clothes and give him the most difficult jobs so that he will be overwhelmed.' I didn't listen to them and answered, 'What's wrong with you? You are not my master and cannot give me orders. I only take orders from Khadija.'"

Hearing the behavior of Abu Jahl and Shayba made Khadija angry. "Was there no one to support you?" she asked.

"Of course," Maysara replied. "Khuzayma supported me and was very annoyed with them."

Khadija was happy that her relative, Khuzayma, had supported Maysara. She gazed at the sky, lost in thought. Coming to herself again, "Please continue, what else happened?" she asked.

Maysara continued, "After selling the goods, we went to the bazaar to buy new goods. Muhammad was bargaining with a salesman and the salesman insisted that he should swear on the idols. He answered, 'I would never swear on the idols. For me, nothing is as unpleasant as they are.' The salesman was confused and couldn't reply. Then, surprisingly, he sold all of his goods to him without bargaining with him."

"You said he didn't swear on the idols, didn't you?" Khadija confirmed.

Nodding, "Yes," Maysara replied.

Hearing this filled Khadija with excitement. "What happened next," she asked.

"The salesman came over to me and, pointing at Muhammad, asked who he was and if I knew him. Then, without waiting for me to answer, he said, 'Never let him go and never stop following him. Surely he is a Prophet.'"

This was exactly what Khadija had wanted to hear. This was the reason she had sent Maysara with the caravan, because he was intelligent enough to observe and remember every detail.

"What else happened?"

"We sold everything and bought new goods. All of this took a long time. Then we set out on our return journey. It was very hot and we needed to rest so we left the main route and looked for somewhere to camp. At the resting place, a monk approached me and introduced himself, "Everyone knows me as the Nestorian monk Bahira. I will swear to you about something. The man sat under that tree is a Prophet.' Then, he went over to Muhammad and spoke to him. 'I swear that you are the noble Prophet foretold in the Gospel. Don't wait here for too long. I am afraid that something evil will happen.'

Finishing his speech, he kissed Muhammad on his forehead."

Everything was exactly as Waraqa had told her. Khadija was lost in thought, 'This is exactly what Waraqa informed me,' she said to herself.

Maysara began to speak again. "When the monk said that the place we rested was not safe, I became afraid. What he said was true, we were at risk from bandits. So, we started our journey again."

Maysara also related that two birds flew over the head of our noble Prophet, peace and blessings be upon him, to shade him from the blazing sun. Furthermore, he explained about the holy light that shone from his forehead, the water that gushed from wherever he stepped when they were thirsty, the food that multiplied when he touched it and the sick camels that recovered when he stroked them.

Khadija was ecstatic by all she heard. She was convinced that he was the last Prophet. She pleaded with Maysara not to relate any of what he had seen and heard to anyone else, and Maysara gave his word.

Khadija visited her cousin, Waraqa, and told him every detail. Waraqa said, "Muhammad will be the last Prophet. There is no doubt about this now."

Blessed Marriage

For two years, Khadija's dreams had indicated that she would marry again. The dreams came one after the other. During this time, she learned a lot about Prophethood and had decided to marry him, but she didn't know how to approach the subject with him.

One day, Nafisa, a close friend of Khadija, was visiting her. Seeing Khadija, she said, "You look so desperate, like you're in pieces. What happened? What is bothering you?"

Khadija remained quiet for a while before answering, "Muhammad, son of Abdullah, has very good manners unlike anyone else. He is the best and most gracious man a woman could ever meet. And, I hear many other good things about him."

Unable to comprehend the intention of her friend, Nafisa replied, "This is very nice and good but what does it have to do with you?"

Mustering up her courage, Khadija came to the point, "I want to marry him. But, I have no idea how I can say this to him."

Understanding her friend's predicament, Nafisa offered, "If you will allow me, I will speak to him and learn his thoughts on this matter."

"If you mean you can help me with this, please do it as soon as possible."

Without wasting any time, Nafisa set out to visit him. Entering the house, he greeted her and asked, "Please, what can I do for you?"

Unable to contain herself, the words almost exploded from Nafisa's mouth, "What is preventing you from marrying?"

Our noble Prophet, peace and blessings be upon him, was not expecting this inquiry. Ashamed and embarrassed his face reddened. He calmly answered, "I am not in a financial position to get married."

"What about if this wasn't a problem? If there was a wealthy woman with honor and beauty, would you marry her?"

Our beloved Prophet understood from this speech that there was a candidate. "Who is she?" he asked.

"Khadija," came the reply.

"How could this be?"

This reply made Nafisa happy. She had the answer she was hoping for. "Let me work it out," she said.

The noble Prophet remained quiet.

Nafisa immediately rushed back to Khadija to let her know what had happened.

Meanwhile, our Prophet consulted his uncle, Abu Talib, about the matter.

After a few days, the uncles of our Prophet, Abu Talib, Abbas and Hamza visited Khadija's relative, Amr ibn Asad to ask his permission for the marriage, in accordance with the local custom of consulting the eldest male.

Khadija was full of excitement. The guests were deep in conversation. All of them were related with each other and this marriage would strengthen the familial bonds between them.

Abu Talib began to speak about the matter at hand, "I am thankful to the Creator that we are descendants of Ismail, son of Abraham." Then, he related the superior characteristics of his nephew and finally announced, "Muhammad wishes to marry Khadija. As a dowry he has promised five hundred dirhams."

Like our noble Prophet, Khadija was also an orphan and was represented by her uncle Amr ibn Asad. He knew that Khadija was favorable to this marriage and so he did not prolong the negotiations. "I agree to the marriage of Khadija, daughter of Khuwaylid with Muhammad, son of Abdullah," he said.

Abu Talib looked at his brothers and said: "I request for you both to witness this marriage."

"We are the witnesses of the marriage of Khadija, daughter of Khuwaylid with Muhammad, son of Abdullah."

They then discussed the date of the wedding celebration.

Khadija, the woman renowned for her wealth, honor and beauty, was now the happiest woman in the world.

Three weeks later, a large and joyful wedding celebration took place with entertainment and a huge banquet. As it came to an end, Khadija said to her new husband, "My dear Muhammad, please tell your uncle, Abu Talib, to sacrifice one or two of your camels and distribute the meat to the people."

Our noble Prophet fulfilled her wish.

Breast Feeding Mother

t forty years old, Khadija finally had a peaceful and happy family.

A short while after the wedding, Khadija was visited by the noble Prophet's wet nurse, the respectable Halima, may Allah be pleased with her. Welcoming her at the door, Khadija hugged her saying, "O my dear mother."

Halima was very affected by Khadija's sincere love towards her and had a comfortable and enjoyable stay in her home. Khadija did her best to fulfill all of Halima's wishes.

One day, Halima told Khadija about her miserable situation. "My animals have all died because of the drought. We are not yet destitute, but our situation is terrible."

"Don't worry mother," Khadija replied. "We will share what we have with you."

Halima was touched by Khadija's good nature and when the time came for them to part, both women's eyes were filled with tears. However, Khadija intended to surprise Halima. Calling one of her servants she said, "Go to the sheepfold and count out forty sheep. Prepare a camel with goods, then give them all to my mother."

Halima was ashamed and refused Khadija's generous gift but Khadija insisted. So, Halima mounted the camel laden with goods and with the forty sheep following behind her, she started her journey home. For our Prophet's wet nurse, this had been an unforgettable visit.

Our noble Prophet had another breastfeeding mother, Thuwayba, may Allah be pleased with her. She was a slave of Abu Lahab and the noble Prophet visited her whenever he could, taking her gifts. She, in turn, visited him often.

One day, whilst our mother Khadija and our noble Prophet were talking, Khadija raised the subject of Thuwayba, saying, "Dear Muhammad, let's buy Thuwayba from Abu Lahab."

He looked at his wife as if to say, "A mother would never be a slave for her son."

Reading his look, Khadija quickly countered, "You misunderstood. We will buy her and give her her freedom."

Delighted with this offer, our noble Prophet was very happy with his wife's consideration. He agreed with the idea.

Lowering to the horizon, the sun was painting the sky with pink and red colors. A beautiful breeze cooled the evening air and the moon was ready to start its night journey to the heavens. Even nature seemed to be applauding these two generous and pure-hearted people with their noble intentions of liberating someone.

Our beloved Prophet and Khadija were excited as they approached Abu Lahab's house. As the door was answered by a servant, they could hear laughter coming from inside. The two holy blessed visitors felt their joy seep away from them, but they could not turn back now.

They entered the room and saw Abu Lahab reclining on thick, soft cushions. Seeing who his guests were, he made a face, indicating his displeasure. After formally greeting each other, Abu Lahab asked, "O son of my brother, you look so oppressed. Did you want something from me?"

Our noble Prophet told his uncle that he wished to buy Thuwayba.

Abu Lahab laughed loudly but at the same time, he was baffled. Standing up from the cushions, wide-eyed, he said, "I know she suckled you and she was your wet nurse and that you love her very much and she loves you, but I will not sell her to you."

All their hopes were in vain. Our Prophet was greatly saddened by Abu Lahab's answer and with hearts full of disappointment they left the house.

Many years later, as the Muslim community immigrated to Medina, Abu Lahab himself liberated Thuwayba.

The First Child

Our beloved Prophet and Khadija were blessed with a baby boy who our noble Prophet named Qasim. Qasim filled their blessed house with joy.

When he was a year old, Qasim couldn't keep still. The little boy's laughter and first baby steps provided hours of enjoyment for his parents. But, when he reached the age of two, Qasim developed a high fever. The maid, Umm Ayman, almost lost her mind seeing Qasim in such a grievous situation. Khadija tried everything to reduce her son's fever but nothing seemed to help. Everyone was filled with fear and dread.

Qasim was so weak they wondered if he would die. No one wanted to believe this could happen. Visitors came and murmured to each other, 'I wonder what disease Qasim has?'

One of the polytheists said, "Probably he was damned by the idols."

A Christian replied, "This could be a hex or black magic."

A woman who was a follower of Abraham's religion suggested, "Could it be that Qasim ate something and it poisoned him?"

Everyone was making assumptions according to their own beliefs.

Just then, an anguished howl emitted from inside the room. Qasim was dead.

This blessed house, normally filled with love, had never known such grief. It was veiled in mourning and everyone was shedding tears. For the first time, the Messenger of Allah understood the pain of losing a child. His tears rained down on the small body. A few hours later, he buried his little son with his own hands.

The child had been so beloved by all, since his birth our noble Prophet had been referred to as Abu'l-Qasim (the father of Qasim).

Our Prophet and Khadija went on to have five more children. Their four daughters, Zaynab, Ruqayyah, Umm Kulthum and Fatima, may Allah be pleased with them, grew into fine women and defenders of the faith. Their son, Abdullah, like his brother Qasim, died in childhood.

Khadija bint Khuwaylid 🌺

You Are My Mother

Zayd ibn Haritha, may Allah be pleased with him, was eight years old when he was kidnapped in Yemen and brought to Mecca. Khadija's nephew bought him as a slave and gave him to Khadija. Later, our Prophet asked her to give him the slave; he wished to liberate him. Khadija accepted this with pleasure.

Little Zayd was very happy now. Khadija treated him like her own son and loved him very much. Everywhere she went, she took Zayd with her and she looked after him, making him special food and buying him many gifts. Zayd became used to being with

45

Khadija and our Prophet and didn't want to leave them.

One day, during the pilgrimage season, some of Zayd's relatives came to visit the Ka'ba. At that time, our noble Prophet, Khadija and Zayd were also there. Recognizing little Zayd, one of his relatives approached, saying, "O Zayd, did you recognize me?"

"Yes, I did," Zayd replied.

"Your father is so sad. He is looking for you everywhere."

Hearing this news, tears started running down Zayd's cheeks. "I know they are looking for me, but they shouldn't be sad anymore. I am in the best hands and am living with the most reliable man in Mecca."

Khadija's throat was choked with emotion. She struggled to fight back her tears. "Dear Zayd," she said, "as you know, you are not a slave. You can go wherever you want."

Zayd looked from Khadija to our Prophet and answered, "You are my parents."

Zayd's relatives were confused. "If Zayd doesn't wish to come back, don't force him to come," they said.

Khadija couldn't bear the thought of a mother crying for her son. She said to Zayd's relatives, "Dear guests of Mecca. Zayd is living with us and he is like our own son. His parents are welcome to come and visit him whenever they wish and Zayd can also visit them whenever he wishes. Please give this message to his parents."

As Zayd's relatives were walking back, Khadija followed them with her eyes, remembering her past. At that time, before she married our Prophet, the garden of her old house was full of children every day. It was like a kindergarten. On one of these days, Khadija's nephew, Hakim ibn Hizam, may Allah be pleased with him, came to see her and asked, "My dear aunt, I am going to the slave market. Is there anything you want?"

"My dear nephew," she replied, "if you find a good slave, please buy him or her for me."

Later that day, Hakim ibn Hizam brought the eight-year old slave, Zayd, to his aunt. Zayd was a lovely child. Khadija warmed to the child instantly. She stroked his head and kissed his forehead. "How did you come to the slave market?" she asked.

As Zayd related his sad story, tears ran down his cheeks. "One day I was visiting a neighbor with my mother. Some bandits came and raided the house. They kidnapped me and brought me to the slave market. They sold me as a slave."

Looking at Zayd, Khadija asked, "Do you love your mother?"

"Of course I love my mother," he replied, wiping away his tears.

Khadija was very sad about his situation. A small child should never be taken away from his parents. She would have to give him back. But how could she find them? He had been kidnapped in Yemen, which was very far away. This wasn't going to be easy.

"Don't worry," she said to little Zayd. "From now on, I'll be your mother and my children are your siblings."

As Zayd's relatives disappeared from sight, Khadija awoke from her daydream. She looked down at Zayd and found he was looking up at her, smiling.

The Guests

One day, Zayd saw two men approaching the house of our Prophet. He recognized them as being his father and his uncle. Zayd ran to his father and after kissing his hand, the two of them embraced emotionally.

The blessed Prophet was watching this scene. He welcomed the guests with a smiling face. They were tired after their long journey.

After being offered refreshments by our noble Prophet, the guests were at a loss of how to thank him. His smiling face and Khadija's wonderful hospitality greatly encouraged them. Haritha, Zayd's father, began to speak, "We came about my son,

Zayd," he said. "Please have compassion for us. Let us pay his ransom and take him home."

Our noble Prophet answered him, "I think just paying the ransom won't solve this problem. Let's think of another way."

"What do you mean?"

"We'll call Zayd and let him make the decision. If he wants to return with you, there is no need to pay a ransom; you can take him. But, if he wants to remain here and chooses me, I wouldn't choose anyone besides him."

Zayd's father and uncle were satisfied with this offer. They thought it would be easy and looked at each other happily. "You found a good solution," said Zayd's uncle.

The blessed Prophet called Zayd and asked him, "Zayd, your father and uncle are requesting for you to return with them. This is the time for farewell. But, the decision is up to you. If you wish to return with them, you can. But, if you wish not to, you can stay here; you know me very well and my compassion for you. It is up to you. You must make your decision now."

All eyes were on Zayd. Speaking with a maturity that belied his young age he said, "I will not forsake you."

Haritha and Zayd's uncle, Qab, could not believe their ears. They were frozen to the spot. A moment later, after his astonishment had passed, Zayd's father said, "O my son, what are you saying? I am your father!"

"Yes, you are my birth father, but..."

"Come to me, son. Here you are a slave, but if you return with me, you will live in freedom."

"Father, here I have always been free."

"Didn't the bandits sell you as a slave? Weren't you bought with money?"

"This is true," Zayd replied, "but from the first day, these people gave me my freedom. I am able to go wherever I want, alone. My life here is very comfortable. Even more so than in your house."

The faces of Zayd's father and uncle paled. They gritted their teeth and trembled with rage. Softly, Zayd spoke again, "Now, my father is Muhammad and my mother is Khadija."

Hearing those words, the men were deflated. They had nothing further to say. Zayd's behavior gave them no hope for his return. Zayd devoted his faithfulness to our Prophet and Khadija. Their care and love for him gave him no wish to return to his parents.

Haritha found this unbearable. "If Zayd loves you that much, he can stay here," he said. Zayd shouted with joy.

The blessed Prophet announced to them all, "You are all witnesses that from now on, Zayd is my own child and my legal inheritor."

A Ladder from the Sky

Our mother Khadija and our noble Prophet had been married for fifteen years. She was fifty-five and he was forty years old. Since the first day of their marriage, their happiness had been increasing day by day.

One night, the blessed Prophet had a dream. He went to Khadija to tell her about it. "A hole opened up in the roof of our house and a silver ladder came down from the sky. From the ladder, two men appeared. I was dumbfounded. Sitting down near me, one of the men plucked my rib from my body and the other, my heart. He said, 'How nice it is, the heart of this righteous man.' Then he washed my heart and put it back into its place. They also replaced my rib, and then they climbed back up the ladder, taking it with them. The roof closed and everything returned to normal."

Khadija listened intently to every word her husband said. "This is a harbinger to you. Allah is sending you blessings."

Khadija had become used to such dreams and knew that in just a short while, her husband would become the last Prophet.

Meanwhile, our noble Prophet was spending hours in devotion to Allah. The idols in the Ka'ba disturbed him greatly, so he often spent his time on the Mountain of Light in the cave of Hira.

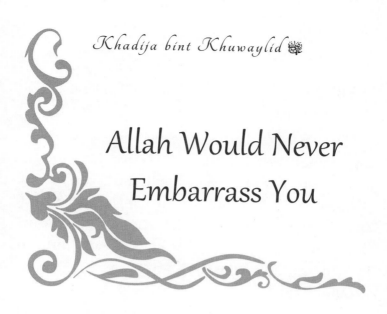

Allah Would Never Embarrass You

One restless night, Khadija was tossing and turning in bed, unable to sleep. Just as she was managing to drift off, she heard a knocking at the door. She thought she was dreaming but the knock continued and she recognized it as her husband's knock. Slowly, she raised herself from the bed and went to open the door. From outside came a beautiful fragrance, such as she had never smelled before.

"Who is it?" she called from inside.

The answer came from her husband and happily she opened the door. When she saw him, she was surprised. He looked different from usual, anxious and distressed. "My dear Muhammad," she said, "You don't look well. What happened? Come and tell me."

In soft tones, he began explaining, "I was walking between the hills, Safa and Marwa, when I heard a voice saying to me, 'O Muhammad, you are the Messenger of Allah and I am Archangel Jibril (Gabriel).' The voice came from heaven, so I raised my head and looked at the sky. There I saw Jibril, in human form. Until he left, I was rooted to the spot. I couldn't move."

Our beloved Prophet was afraid that what he had seen could have been the devil or something else sinister. "I am so afraid. Maybe the devil is turning me into a soothsayer. But I have never liked idols or soothsayers."

Khadija was smiling. "My dear Muhammad. Don't worry. I can see a light on your face that I have never seen before," she reassured him.

The blessed Prophet continued, "Dear Khadija, I also hear voices and see lights. On the way to our house, voices were greeting me but there was no one around, only trees and stones."

Seeing that she hadn't manage to reassure our Prophet, Khadija tried again to calm him. "Allah would never embarrass you," she said. "You treat your relatives very well, help the needy and protect the poor. You come to the aid of the aggrieved and you are a wonderful host to your guests."

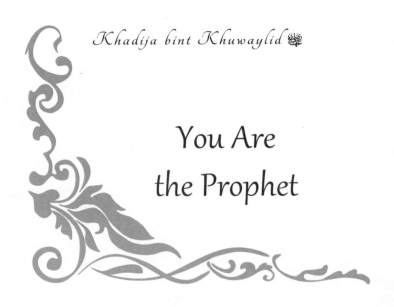

You Are
the Prophet

*I*n those days, our noble Prophet was spending a lot of time in the desert, submitting himself in devotion to Allah. The clarity of the desert sky, the vastness of the land and the peace and silence of the cave of Hira made his heart expand with joy. He constantly felt the pull of the Mountain of Light.

Hugging his children whom he referred to as "the light of my eyes", and taking leave of his wife, he left to return to the mountain. His children and Khadija watched him until he was out of sight. Then, Khadija returned to her chores, completing them without her husband by her side.

When night fell, people returned to their homes and the doors were locked. Khadija spent time chatting to her children, and then everyone retired to bed. For Khadija it was another sleepless night.

Just as dawn was breaking, as the sun lifted its head over the horizon of Mecca, a knock was heard gently tapping at the door. Everyone in the household heard the knock and looked at each other questioningly. One child said, "This is our father. He always knocks at the door!"

"Absolutely," replied another.

But, none of them really believed their father would return at this time of the day.

Jumping up from her bed, Khadija ran and opened the door without asking who it was. When she saw her husband she was filled with joy but this time, he looked even more unusual. He was trembling like a leaf. As soon as he entered the house, he cried out to be covered with a blanket.

Khadija immediately rushed to fulfill his wishes. "Dear Muhammad, I could sacrifice everything for you. What has happened," she entreated her husband.

"Whilst I was praying in the cave on the mountain, a bright light illuminated the space and I saw a beautiful person in front of me. He was robed in embroidered satin and emitted the most wonderful fragrance. He said to me, 'Read!' I answered that I cannot read. After this, he hugged me, squeezing me so powerfully I thought I would die. He repeated, 'Read!' and again, I answered that I cannot read. He hugged and squeezed me again. This happened three times. Then, he said:

> Read in and with the Name of your Lord, Who has created—Created human from a clot clinging (to the wall of the womb). Read, and your Lord is the All-Munificent, Who has taught (human) by the pen—Taught human what he did not know. (Al-Alaq 96:1–5).

I repeated all of his words and then he disappeared."

Khadija was captivated by our Prophet's words. "This is again a harbinger my dear Muhammad. Don't be afraid of the place you were staying. I swear you are the long-awaited Prophet. I know this for sure, but, I will ask my cousin Waraqa about your experience."

Khadija left the house and rushed to report the news to Waraqa ibn Nawfal. When he heard what had passed he was filled with excitement. "He is a Prophet. Go and tell him this news. I want to see him as soon as possible."

Later, Waraqa and the blessed Prophet met in the yard of the Ka'ba.

"Please, dear Muhammad," Waraqa said. "Tell me everything that happened. I want to hear it directly from you."

Starting from the beginning, our Prophet told him everything. As he listened to the events that had passed in the cave, Waraqa repeatedly said, "Allah is Almighty."

Addressing our Prophet, he said, "It was Jibril that came to you. He is the angel of revelation and he also came to Moses and Jesus. I swear that you are the last Prophet foretold in the Gospel."

Listening to them both, Khadija's eyes flickered with joy as if reflecting the light of a candle. Could there be anything more honorable than being the wife of a Prophet?

His eyes filled with tears, Waraqa said, "I wish I was younger so that I could be at your side when your nation expels you from here."

When she heard these words, Khadija froze but our noble Prophet asked calmly, "Will I be expelled from Mecca?"

Waraqa spoke with assurance, "Yes, they will accuse you of being a liar. They will harm you and force you to leave your land. The worst thing is that they will fight against you. Every Prophet has suffered the cruelty of his nation."

Who Would Ever Listen to Me?

*A*fter receiving the first revelation, our Prophet frequently visited the cave of Hira and waited for Jibril. Khadija, like her blessed husband, was also waiting eagerly.

On the fortieth night, as he was returning from the mountain, our Prophet heard a voice in the valley. It was a familiar voice that he had heard many times before. Looking up at the sky, he saw Jibril with his wings spread across the whole horizon. It was a spectacular scene. The angel was sitting on a pedestal suspended between heaven and earth. At that moment, our Prophet felt the entire weight of the world on his shoulders and fainted from the pressure. Coming round a while later, he stood and began to walk home.

As he walked he encountered something strange. All the stones and the trees greeted him saying, "Peace be with you, O Messenger of Allah."

The entire nature and cosmos were greeting him and offering their congratulations on his Prophethood. By the time he arrived home, he was speechless from the excitement and strangeness of what was happening.

Khadija had been waiting for a herald, but, when she saw our noble Prophet in this state, she was shocked. Again he requested to be covered with a blanket.

Khadija covered her blessed husband with a blanket and sat with his head resting on her knee. He was in a dreamlike state and remained like that for a while. His forehead broke out in beads of sweat and Khadija was afraid he had caught a fever. Suddenly, our Prophet stood up and said, "Allah is the greatest." Khadija couldn't understand what had happened, but in fact, at that moment, Jibril had appeared to our Prophet and revealed,

O you enwrapped one, (under the heavy respon-
sibility of Messengership)! Rise to keep vigil at
night, except a little; half of it, or lessen it a little; or add to it (a little). And pray and recite the
Qur'an calmly and distinctly (with your mind
and heart concentrated on it). (Al-Muzzammil
73:1–4).

Our Prophet and Khadija understood that this
was a clear revelation. He was calmer than he had
been after the first revelation when Jibril had ordered
him to read. However, the meaning of the new revelation exhausted him.

Looking at his beloved wife he said, "Dear Khadija, there is no rest for me. Jibril told me to warn the
people and invite them to worship Allah. But, who
will listen to me?"

Without hesitating, Khadija answered, "I'll listen to you. I'll be the first believer in your religion."

Both of them testified and Khadija became the
first Muslim.

From that day onwards, our Prophet spent more
and more time on the Mountain of Light, some days
returning home very late. Khadija supported her hus-

band by preparing food and taking it to him in the cave of Hira.

On one of those days, Jibril visited the blessed Prophet saying, "Here comes Khadija. She is bringing you food and drink. When she comes here give her greetings from Allah and from me and tell her the good news that she has a place in Paradise."

When Khadija arrived at the cave, our Prophet gave her the message from Jibril.

"For sure, this is a greeting from Allah," Khadija said. "May Allah's blessings be upon Jibril. May Allah's blessings and compassion be upon you. May His blessings be upon everyone except the Devil."

She Was the First at Everything

Our noble Prophet continued to receive the revelations from Allah. One day, Jibril appeared in a valley above Mecca and approached the Messenger of Allah. Striking the ground with his heel, water spread all around them. Our Prophet looked at him curiously.

Jibril bent down and washed his hands, up to his elbows. Then, he took some water into his mouth and washed it. After this, he sniffed water into his nose and washed his face. He put his wet hand on his head and wiped behind his ears, then, lastly, he washed his feet. The blessed Prophet repeated all of Jibril's actions and therefore, completed his ablution for the Daily Ritual Prayers for the first time.

Having made their ablution, our dear Prophet and Jibril prayed together. The Messenger of Allah was very happy. He had received Allah's instruction to pray which he had been eagerly awaiting. Suffused with a deep sense of faith and joy he returned home to tell Khadija what had happened. He took her to the well and taught her how to wash for the Daily Prayer, then they prayed together.

Speaking with Jibril

K hadija was one of the few people that understood the noble Prophet well. Without him even speaking, she could sense what he wanted or needed just by looking into his eyes. When he was sad, she shared his sadness and when he was happy she was happy too. Whenever people disturbed him, she was his comfort.

When the revelations became more frequent, the polytheists started to gossip and suggested it could be the work of the devil. This saddened our Prophet. Hearing this rumors again one day, our Prophet became distressed and went to find Khadija. She assured him that he was seeing Jibril, not the devil.

"Can you let me know when Jibril visits you here?" she asked.

"Yes, I will inform you when he comes to speak with me."

Whilst receiving her education from Waraqa, Khadija had learned the characteristics of Jibril from him. She knew that no one except the blessed Prophet could see him which is why she asked him for news when he came.

A while later, Jibril came to speak with our noble Prophet and Khadija was given the news that he was present. She asked our noble Prophet to sit on one of her knees. The Messenger of Allah did as she requested. "Is he still here?" Khadija asked.

"Yes," replied the Messenger of Allah.

Then she asked our Prophet to sit on her other knee. When the Messenger of Allah sat on both of her knees, she asked again, "Can you still see him?"

"Yes, I can see him."

Khadija slid her scarf a little from her head and asked again, "Can you see him now?"

This time, the answer was negative, "No he isn't here anymore. I can't see him."

Khadija cried out with joy, "O Muhammad! This is a sign for you. I swear that this is an angel and not the devil. The devil has no sense of shame. Even if I completely removed my scarf he wouldn't be embarrassed and would remain sitting here."

Thanks to his dear wife, the beloved Prophet was relieved again.

Competition of Devotion

Over the next three years, the Messenger of Allah tirelessly invited people to Islam and his wife, Khadija, was one of his greatest helpers. She made huge sacrifices to win peoples' hearts and told many women about the Islamic religion. She prepared sumptuous banquets and helped many people to become Muslim. Along with Abu Bakr, may Allah be pleased with him, she worked very hard to spread the religion. The two blessed friends acted as if they were in a competition of devotion and the Islamic religion became the main topic of conversation between people in Mecca.

Day by day, the number of Muslims increased, reaching forty after six years. By the time Umar, may Allah be pleased with him, converted to Islam, everyone in Mecca had heard about the new religion. Abu Bakr, Zayd, and Uthman, may Allah be pleased with them, were inviting people from every corner of the city to this religion.

The spread of the new religion filled the polytheists leaders with fear that the Muslims would become powerful and they began to torture them. The level of torture increased day by day and came to the attention of Abu Talib. He called together two of the main tribes in Mecca to protect the Muslims. The tribes accepted the offer and the Quraysh polytheists were powerless against them.

Frustrated by the protection offered to the Muslims, the Quraysh increased their efforts to make life impossible for them and decided to start a boycott. They wrote an agreement on paper and hung it on the wall of the Ka'ba. The terms of the agreement were very harsh for the Muslims and it became the cause of great sadness for the Messenger of Allah.

The noble Prophet's uncle, Abu Talib, was also sorry about this decision of the Quraysh polytheists.

He told them that their agreement would bring them disaster and advised them to have mercy on the Muslims and not forget their ties of kinship and friendship. It would be better for everyone to live together in peace.

The boycott lasted for three years. The polytheists held the Muslims in detention and blocked their access to the market and public places. No food or drink was allowed through to the Muslim neighborhoods.

The sounds of starving children crying could be heard for miles. The Muslims were only permitted to travel freely in the city during the pilgrimage season, and even then, could only provide for their needs from the local market, being forbidden to trade with other cities. Abu Lahab, one of the biggest enemies of the Muslims, encouraged the traders to charge extra high prices, saying, "O traders, charge high prices to the friends of Muhammad. Do not give them the chance to buy anything."

Everyone was afraid of Abu Lahab and no one had the courage to disobey him. They knew they would suffer if they went against his wishes and so they raised their prices. Unable to afford anything in the market, the Muslims usually returned to their poor children empty-handed.

During the boycott, Khadija gave all her wealth to aid the poor and needy, ending up in a state of starvation herself. Hearing about her terrible situation, her relatives tried to help her secretly.

One day, Khadija's nephew, Hakim, prepared some wheat and set out to take it to his aunt. As he was about to enter Muslim territory he was stopped by Abu Jahl, "You are bringing food to the Muslims?" he shouted.

Hakim was surprised and speechless. Abu Jahl was furious. He shouted at Hakim and harassed him badly. Hakim's faced paled. As more polytheists surrounded him, he was afraid of being lynched and feared for his life.

"As long as I live here, you will neither enter Muslim territory, nor will you bring them food. If you do, I will humiliate you in front of all of Mecca," Abu Jahl yelled.

At that moment, Hisham, another friend and supporter of Khadija, arrived. Abu Jahl complained, "Look, he also brings food to the Muslims!"

But, rather than being intimidated, Hisham roared like a lion, "How can you stop someone from bringing food to his own aunt?"

Speaking firmly he said, "Move away and let the man go where he wants to go."

Abu Jahl wasn't ready to back down. He wouldn't allow Hakim to pass and continued to harass him. Unable to hold himself back, Hisham picked up a camel jawbone from the ground and clutching it tightly, smashed Abu Jahl on the head.

The man who, just a moment ago, had been bellowing like a dinosaur was now writhing in pain on the ground. Hisham kicked Abu Jahl in the back as he begged for mercy. He could no longer look at the faces of the people gathered around him.

* * *

When the polytheists wrote the boycott agreement that was hung on the wall of the Ka'ba, the word "Allah" was written at the beginning. Over time, worms had eaten the agreement and the only word left untouched was "Allah". This didn't go unnoticed. Abu Talib gained confidence from the event with Abu Jahl and shouted courageously at

the polytheists, "Are you still not aware of what you have done? All that cruelty, mischief and evil?"

Some of the more compassionate polytheists realized what he was implying and agreed to end the boycott.

By the end of the three-year boycott, Khadija, who was once one of Mecca's wealthiest women, was destitute. She had distributed all of her belongings among the Muslims to support them through those long and difficult years. She herself was now in need and her relatives were very upset by her condition. However, this blessed woman was never happier than when she was by the side of her beloved Prophet.

The Year of Sadness

Three years of intense struggle and poverty had weakened Khadija. Her body had been ravaged by disease causing her to lose a lot of weight. She was sick and unable to recover. The noble Prophet was distraught by her condition. No one had seen him this sad before. Tears ran unchecked down his cheeks and his words stuck in his throat.

"My dear Khadija," he wept, "You have suffered so much because of me."

Khadija had no power to answer him with words but she tried to contradict him with her eyes.

"I could not give you the good life you deserved. O Khadija, you couldn't live a comfortable life, but those who have been burned once will not burn again. Allah has promised beautiful rewards for you after so much suffering."

The blessed Prophet kept vigil over his wife for days and nights reading the Qur'an and praying for her. On the twenty-seventh day of Ramadan, Khadija, loyal wife of our Prophet and the mother of all mothers, flew like a bird to Paradise.

Khadija had spent twenty-five of her sixty-five years with the Messenger of Allah. His grief could not be explained with words. His most loyal companion, his adoring wife, was no longer there.

The noble Prophet prepared himself to perform his last duty for his beloved wife. He buried her in Mecca's cemetery and read her Funeral Prayer.

Three days after Khadija's death, the noble Prophet suffered another devastating loss. Abu Talib, the noble Prophet's uncle, close friend and protector died. He had been the blessed Prophet's right arm, an excellent helper and loyal friend. He gave everything he had to the poverty-stricken Muslims during the boycott years and showed great sacrifice.

Losing two essential companions within three days was almost too much for the Messenger of Allah. He was inconsolable. "Two terrible misfortunes afflicting my community, I don't know which one makes me more upset."

He named this year, "The Year of Sadness."